# CAT CASTLES

# CAT CASTLES

## 20 Cardboard Habitats
## You Can Build Yourself

Carin Oliver

QUIRK BOOKS
PHILADELPHIA

First published in the United States in 2016
by Quirk Productions, Inc

Quirk Books
215 Church St.
Philadelphia, PA 19106
www.quirkbooks.com

Library of Congress Cataloging in
Publication Number: 2016930954
ISBN: 978-1-59474-941-4

Conceived, edited, and designed by
Marshall Editions
The Old Brewery
6 Blundell Street
London N7 9BH
UK
www.quartoknows.com

Senior Editor: Lily de Gatacre
Art Editor and Designer: Jackie Palmer
Photographers: Liz Coleman and
    Phil Wilkins
Illustrator: Olya Kamieshkova
Proofreader: Caroline West
Indexer: Helen Snaith
Art Director: Caroline Guest

Creative Director: Moira Clinch
Publisher: Paul Carslake

Printed in China

**Safety first!** The author and publisher
assume no responsibility for the results of
these projects, nor for any loss or damage
that might result from their use. Choose
your cat-friendly materials wisely, and
make sure your cat's furniture is secured
and in good condition. Although it makes
for amazing photos, a cardboard ship will
not allow your cat to set sail on water.

# Contents

Cats have figured out what's important: a little place to call their own, a good perch from which to survey their domain, and a comfy place to take a nap followed by a nice stretch. But although they are great at snoozing, napping, lazing, taking it easy, drowsing, dozing, lolling, lounging, loafing, idling, unwinding, resting, hanging loose, and hanging out, they are not great at arts and crafts. That's where you come in.

# INTRODUCTION

If you **share your home** with a cat, then you know that cats are **experts** at relaxing.

The projects presented here are hideouts, lounges, and accessories that you can make yourself and customize to your and your cat's liking. Sure, you could go to a pet store and purchase accessories for your cat, but making them yourself has several benefits: you get the pleasure of making something with your hands, you save money—particularly if you use materials you have around the house—and you can create something unique that suits you and your cat perfectly.

Creating custom items for your feline friends is a great way to bond with them and get to know them better. To make a hangout that is ideally suited for your cat, you will have to consider not only physical elements, like size, but also personality traits and preferences. Does your cat like to snooze in dark spaces? Or would she rather be perched on top of a stack of boxes? Once you build a project and let your cat try it out, you can continue to change and customize it:

doors can be made bigger, windows installed, pillows added. Hopefully, once you've built a few of these projects, you'll be inspired to create cat castles of your own design.

## When did it all begin?

Cats have been human companions for thousands of years. It is believed that cats first wandered into human settlements when people began farming and storing grain. The grain attracted rodents, and the rodents attracted cats, who made themselves useful by exterminating the rodents. Although it may have started out utilitarian, nowadays the human–feline relationship is different. Most house cats live pampered lives, with no requirement that they earn their keep. They do still provide benefits to us—less tangible yet much needed ones: comfort, companionship, and love.

## Design tips

- **Make it the right size.** Before you start making projects, see what size space your cat likes to hang out in by offering her three boxes of different sizes with doors cut in them. You can also test to find your cat's preferred door size by cutting the options into an old box.

- **Make it sturdy.** If you have a particularly large cat, it's a good idea to use double-thick corrugated cardboard for weight-bearing components.

- **Make it safe.** When decorating projects, don't use anything that your cat could swallow, such as glitter, sequins, or beads.

- **Make it beautiful.** Cats don't see colors the same way humans do, and they likely don't care if their new hideout matches your couch. The decorating is for you, so take the opportunity to customize in a way that reflects your style.

- **Make it comfortable.** Adding a blanket or pillow and a favorite toy or two are great finishing touches that will make kitty feel comfy and at home.

# TOOLS and MATERIALS

All the tools and materials needed to make these **cat hangouts** are inexpensive and easy to come by—that's the **beauty** of it. You'll probably find that you already have many of these items around the house, and the rest can be found at a hardware or craft-supply store.

## Materials

### Corrugated cardboard

This is the primary material you'll use in the construction of your cat hangouts. You can buy sheets online or from craft or office-supply stores, or you can cut up boxes that you have around the house.

### Cardboard

If you need thinner cardboard (the non-corrugated kind) or just small amounts, you can buy sheets of cardstock at craft stores or cut out sections from packing boxes or food containers such as cereal boxes.

### Cardboard boxes

From file-storage boxes with lids to enormous packing cartons, cardboard boxes are the perfect foundation for creating cat hangouts. You can make exciting and solid structures easily—with a few tweaks, a bit of imagination, and the right decoration. Start collecting all the boxes you find or head down to your local office-supply store to stock up. Just make sure that any box you choose as the basis of a project is big enough for your cat to comfortably hang out in.

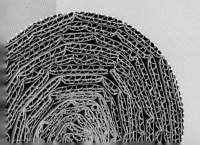

## Small cardboard boxes

Empty tissue boxes or cardboard food containers are ideal for adding embellishments and details to your cardboard structures. Be sure to remove any plastic or non-cat-friendly materials from the box.

## Cardboard tubes

These are typically used as concrete forms but are great for making tubular cat hangouts—and avoiding the tricky task of trying to create a tube out of flat cardboard. They're available online and at building-supply stores. Shipping tubes are a great option if you want a cardboard tube that doesn't need to be big enough to fit a cat.

## Toilet-paper tubes

Plain cardboard tubes can add all sorts of interesting details to your hangouts.

## Sisal rope

Cats need to scratch to keep their claws in shape and stretch their muscles. This natural fiber is easily found at craft and hardware stores and is perfect for scratching. Make sure it is plain and not coated with oils or anything else.

## Twine

This is a really useful addition to many projects and great fun for your cat to play with. Stick to a natural fiber such as sisal.

## Bamboo skewers

These are easy to find in your local grocery store, and they often come in a range of large and small sizes.

## Wooden dowels

Bigger and sturdier than bamboo skewers, these come in many different sizes. Available at craft stores.

## Plywood

You may want to add a little structure in addition to cardboard. Plywood is inexpensive, easy to work with, and readily available at garden centers and hardware stores.

## Tape

Use masking or painter's tape to temporarily hold parts together while glue dries or to close up the tops or bottoms of cardboard boxes before construction.

## Nontoxic glue

Nontoxic hot glue is a good choice for the construction of the cat hangouts since it is easy to use and dries quickly. Just be sure to remove any glue blobs that remain— you don't want your cat to eat these. For some of the projects, you'll need nontoxic wood glue. Choose a nontoxic craft glue or glue stick for adding embellishments or construction-paper decoration.

## Heavy wire

You can either use wire from a coat hanger or thinner wire from the hardware store.

## Pencil

It's always handy to have a few well-sharpened pencils on hand for drawing shapes or marking points for cutting.

## Decorative paper

Construction paper and wrapping paper come in every color and pattern you can think of and are easy to find. Paper is the perfect material to decorate your hangouts quickly and easily without using messy paints or spending hours drawing with markers.

## Nontoxic paint

Water-based, nontoxic craft paints are great for decorating cardboard and come in every color of the rainbow!

## Nontoxic markers

Add finer details with water-based, nontoxic markers.

## Felt

Try decorating your projects with colored felt for an extra-warm and cozy hangout.

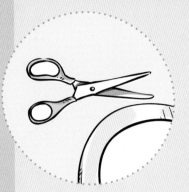

# Tools

### Long steel ruler

Your craft projects will always turn out best if your measurements are accurate. It's especially important if you are creating a door between two or more openings.

### Measuring tape

If you are making a really large project or have to measure around a shape or corner, for example, a measuring tape can be more useful than a ruler.

### Utility knife

This is the best tool for cutting corrugated cardboard and cardboard boxes. The blades are very sharp, so use them with care.

### Hot-glue gun

These are easy to use, accurate, and mess-free! You can find small, inexpensive models in craft or art-supply stores. The glue is hot as it comes out of the gun, so keep the nozzle away from your skin and never let a child use one without supervision. Remember to unplug your hot-glue gun and rest it on a safe surface out of reach. Remove any glue "strings" that might be left behind so your cat doesn't eat them.

### Scissors

A good, sturdy pair works best for cutting cardboard.

### Wire cutters

If you're using wire, it's important to use the right tools to snip it. You can find these cutters at hardware stores. Note that some pliers have a wire cutter built in.

### Pliers

Use these for bending and twisting wire, particularly when working with thick wire that is not easy to bend or shape by hand.

### Hand saw

This is the best tool for cutting sticks and dowels. It should be handled with care and used only on an appropriate, sturdy, and supported surface.

## Paintbrushes

It's useful to have a few paintbrushes in several different, small sizes. Use them for painting or applying glue.

## Sewing needle

You may need to create a small hole in a piece of cardboard, and this is the ideal tool to help you do that.

## Rolling pin

Cardboard is flexible and can be bent to your needs. Use a rolling pin or other tubular structure to turn a flat piece of cardboard into a curved shape.

## Drill and drill bit

A drill is important for adding wooden elements to your projects, such as the wooden base of the scratching post on pages 84–85.

The **projects** in this book are **easy to make** and contain **full instructions** that will guide you from **beginning** to end. However, there are a few **common techniques** to **familiarize yourself** with before you begin.

# BASIC TECHNIQUES

## Scoring and folding

Making a clean fold in cardboard—especially thick, corrugated cardboard—can be tricky. Taking your time and doing an extra step or two will improve the final project.

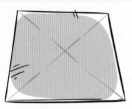

**1** / Working on the side of the cardboard that will be the outside of the folded shape, use a ruler to measure and draw a line where you'd like the fold to be.

**2** / Place a long steel ruler along the line. Using a utility knife and gentle pressure, lightly score a line across the surface. Be careful not to cut all the way through.

**3** / Flip the cardboard over and then measure and draw a line in the same place. Lay the ruler on the line and fold up the cardboard, bending along the line you scored in Step 2. The result will be a crisp, accurate fold.

## Cutting with a utility knife

A utility knife or craft knife is a great option for cutting cardboard, especially pieces that are too big or too thick for scissors. Always be careful when working with sharp blades.

**1** / Protect your work surface with a cutting mat or scrap piece of cardboard. Self-healing cutting mats are ideal and can be found in most craft and art-supply stores.

**2** / If the knife has a locking blade, make sure that it is locked securely in place before use. When cutting, keep your other hand out of the path of the blade.

**3** / When cutting a straight line, use a steel ruler. Your blade will cut into plastic or wooden rulers, leaving them uneven. Hold the ruler in place with your non-cutting hand, keeping your fingers well away from the blade.

**4** / To cut curves or circles, move the cardboard around as you go so that the blade is always cutting toward you and you are not bending in unnatural ways!

**5** / Cut using gentle pressure and make several passes, if necessary. Always pull the blade toward you; never try to push it away from you.

**6** / Always retract or cover the blade when you have finished cutting.

# Cutting a tube

Cutting a cardboard tube can be done with a utility knife or small hand saw. You can't use a ruler to keep a straight line, so follow these steps to ensure accuracy.

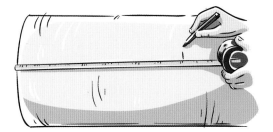

**1** / Measure and mark the correct cutting point in several places around the tube.

**2** / Connect the cutting marks with a length of tape, making a straight line around the tube.

**3** / Use a hand saw or utility knife to cut along this line. It is easier if you rotate the tube periodically so you are always cutting on the top of the tube.

# Using a hot-glue gun

The most important thing to remember when gluing is to wait for the glue to set before moving on to the next stage of construction. This is particularly important for complex or multilevel hangouts.

**1** Protect the work surface with a scrap piece of paper or cardboard. It's also a good idea to have a scrap piece of card to set the gun on when not in use to catch any drips of glue.

**2** Insert the glue stick, following the instructions on the glue gun, and turn on. Let the glue gun warm up fully before you begin (usually 5-10 minutes).

**3** Hold the gun right next to the area you want to glue, gently pull the trigger, and move the gun to apply the glue. Release the trigger and move the tip of the gun sideways to break any "strings" of glue between the gun and the surface. Be sure to remove all the little glue "strings" so that your cat doesn't end up accidentally eating them.

**4** When you've finished gluing, unplug the glue gun immediately. Always keep the glue gun in an upright position while it is hot.

Safety tip: Hot glue is hot! Keep it away from cats and kids, and never touch the nozzle or molten glue with unprotected fingers.

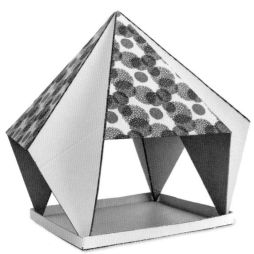

pages 44-47

pages 48-51

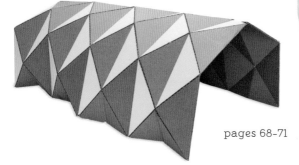

pages 68-71

If you've got more than one cat, keep them all happy with the Nap Tubes or Stepped Condo.

pages 80-83

pages 72-75

pages 24-27

pages 34-37

# Projects

In this section you'll find instructions and ideas for 20 cardboard habitats and projects to delight both you and your cat.

The Castle is great if you want to flex those creative muscles.

pages 20-23

pages 28-29

pages 52-54

pages 84-85

Looking for a quick and easy project? Try the Cat Headquarters.

pages 60-61

pages 62-65

pages 30-33

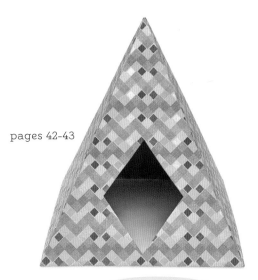

pages 42-43

pages 56-59

Fill the Pyramid or Geo Pod with cushions or blankets for a cozy cat den.

The Hanging Scratching Pad will save your furniture from kitty's claws.

pages 66-67

pages 76-79

pages 86-91

pages 38-41

Almost **any** collection of **boxes** can become a **palace** fit for **feline royalty.**

CASTLE

## Tools & Materials

Several cardboard boxes, some of them large enough for your cat to hang out in

Corrugated cardboard for details

Tape

Long steel ruler

Pencil

Utility knife

Glue and/or hot-glue gun

Sisal twine

2 bamboo skewers

Construction paper

Optional: paintbrush and paint or decorative paper

**1** / Decide on a basic layout for your castle and arrange the boxes. A small rectangular box might work well for the gatehouse, which will be the entry. To make towers, use tall boxes or stack two or more cubes. Here, we'll create a simple castle with a gatehouse and two towers. Tape all of the boxes closed.

**2** / Draw a door in the gatehouse. Make sure it is large enough for your cat to fit through easily. You can use a ruler to ensure the sides are straight, if you wish.

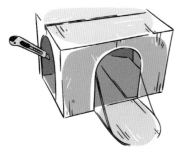

**3** / Cut out the top and sides of the door shape. Leave the bottom uncut to serve as a hinge. Pull the door open to create a drawbridge.

**4** / Glue one end of a piece of twine to the left edge of the drawbridge and the other end to the left of the doorway opening. Repeat on the right side. These are the chains that would pull up the drawbridge.

**5** / Cut doors on each side of the gatehouse where you want to connect the towers.

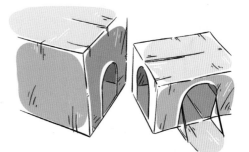

**6** / Cut matching doors in the base of the towers, making sure they are the same size and shape.

**7** / If your towers have a second level, cut matching holes in the "ceiling" of the first level and the "floor" of the second level so your cat can get up and down.

**8** / Add doors to the second level of your towers.

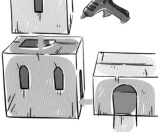

**9** / Cut some small windows in your towers so your cat can peek out.

**10** / Glue the first and second floors of the towers together and then glue them onto the gatehouse. Make sure that all the doorways align so that your cat doesn't get stuck.

**12** /

For a finishing touch, poke a bamboo skewer into the top of each tower. Cut flags out of construction paper and glue to the top of each skewer. Your castle can be left as it is or further embellished with paint or decorative paper.

**11** / To make ramparts, cut strips of corrugated cardboard and cut out square notches along one side. Glue these to the tops of the gatehouse and around the top of each section of the towers.

As your cat's empire expands, her castle can expand, too—just add more boxes.

For the true **daredevil** feline, only an aircraft will do!

# AIRPLANE

## Tools & Materials

Cardboard box large enough for your cat to sit in

Corrugated cardboard for details

Utility knife

Tape

Pencil

Glue and/or hot-glue gun

Short length of heavy wire

Wire cutters

Pliers

Optional: paintbrush and paint or decorative paper

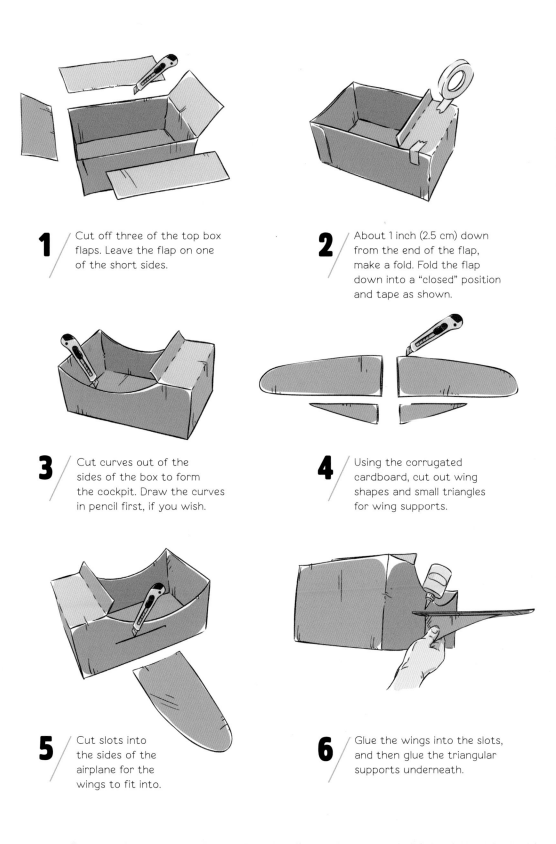

**1** Cut off three of the top box flaps. Leave the flap on one of the short sides.

**2** About 1 inch (2.5 cm) down from the end of the flap, make a fold. Fold the flap down into a "closed" position and tape as shown.

**3** Cut curves out of the sides of the box to form the cockpit. Draw the curves in pencil first, if you wish.

**4** Using the corrugated cardboard, cut out wing shapes and small triangles for wing supports.

**5** Cut slots into the sides of the airplane for the wings to fit into.

**6** Glue the wings into the slots, and then glue the triangular supports underneath.

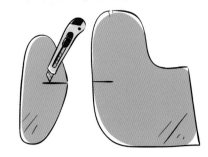

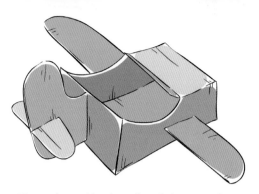

**7** / Using the corrugated cardboard, cut out shapes for the tail of the plane, and add slots as shown to fit them together.

**8** / Assemble the tail and glue together. Cut a slot in the back of the plane, insert the tail, and glue. You may want to decorate the box now.

**9** / Cut out a propeller shape and two small discs from the corrugated cardboard. Use the wire to poke a hole in the center of each. Decorate if desired.

**10** / Use the wire to poke a hole in the front of the plane for the propeller.

**11** / Thread the propeller onto the wire, followed by the two discs. Insert the wire into the hole in the front of the plane.

**12** / Trim the wire if necessary and bend each end over with pliers to hold the propeller on. Now watch your feline aviator take off on an adventure!

This is a really fun project to decorate, and it's ideal for taking whimsical photos of your cat!

There's no **question** about whose hideout **this is.**

# CAT HEADQUARTERS

**Tools & Materials**

Cardboard box large enough for your cat to hang out in
Pencil
Utility knife
Small blanket or pillow

**1** Select a box that is just the right size for your cat—not too big, not too small.

**2** Draw a doorway in the shape of a cat's head or any other shape you want.

**3** Carefully cut out the doorway.

Add a blanket, small pillow, or your cat's favorite toy to make the Cat HQ comfy.

Feed your **feline's** entrepreneurial **spirit** by setting him up with a **restaurant** on **wheels.**

# FOOD TRUCK

## Tools & Materials

Large cardboard box, large enough for your cat to fit inside when closed

Corrugated cardboard for details

Tape

Utility knife

Long steel ruler

Pencil

Glue and/or hot-glue gun

Scissors

Optional: paintbrush and paint or markers

·Menu·

**1** Tape the box closed. Cut a notch out of the front to create the front of the truck.

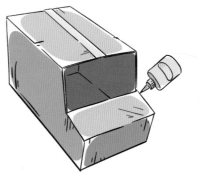

**2** Measure and cut a piece of corrugated cardboard for the hood and glue or tape it onto the front.

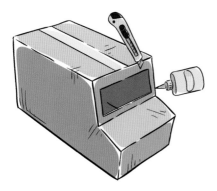

**3** Measure and cut a piece of corrugated cardboard for the windshield and cut out the middle. Glue or tape it in place.

**4** Draw and cut out two front side windows.

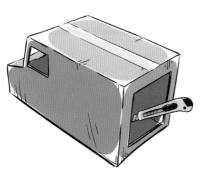

**5** Cut out most of the back side to make a door. Make sure it's big enough for your cat to comfortably fit through.

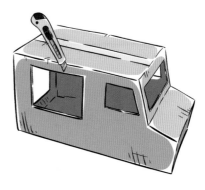

**6** Cut out the service window.

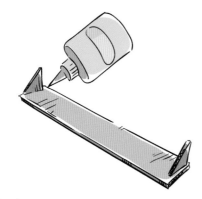

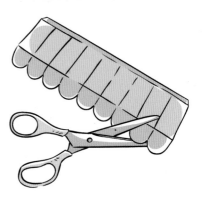

**7** / To make a counter, cut a strip of corrugated cardboard the same width as the service window, and add a right-angled triangle at each end to act as supports.

**8** / Make an awning by cutting a rectangle of corrugated cardboard slightly wider than the service window. Score and fold down a strip along each long side, about 1 inch (2.5 cm) from the edge. If you like, cut scallops or another decorative pattern into one edge.

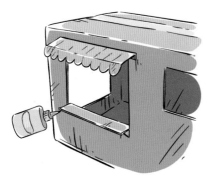

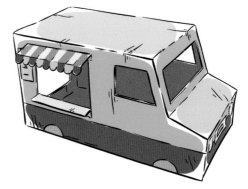

**9** / Glue on the counter at the bottom of the service window, and glue the back tab of the awning just above the window.

**10** / If you like, decorate the truck with paint or markers. Be sure to post a special menu featuring your cat's highest profit-generating favorites.

Cats need to **scratch** to keep their **claws** trim. Save **your** furniture by giving your kitty this **easy**-to-make scratching pad.

# ROUND SCRATCHING PAD

**Tools & Materials**

Large pieces of corrugated cardboard (use double-thickness if you can find it—it will save you time)
Long steel ruler
Pencil
Utility knife
Painter's tape
Felt or decorative paper
Glue
Optional: catnip

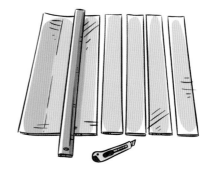

**1** Measure 4-inch (10-cm) wide strips of corrugated cardboard. The ridges of the cardboard should run perpendicular to the long side so that they will bend easily.

**2** Cut out lots of these strips.

**3** Take one of the strips and fold the end over, then roll it up tightly around itself. When you reach the end, tape it down with painter's tape.

**4** Continue winding and taping more strips around this central spiral until you reach the diameter desired for your scratching pad.

**5** For the outside, cut a strip of felt or decorative paper, 4 inches (10 cm) wide and long enough to wrap all the way around the scratching pad. Glue it into place.

Sprinkle catnip on the pad to drive your cat wild. To keep the catnip from falling through and onto the floor, glue a circle of felt or paper to the bottom of the pad.

35 | ROUND SCRATCHING PAD

The scratching pad will double as a platform on which your cat may choose to survey her kingdom.

Your **cat** can
**set sail** for **adventure**
and **conquest** on
the **high seas.**

# PIRATE SHIP

## Tools & Materials

Corrugated cardboard
for the body of the ship
Thin cardboard for sails
Pencil
Utility knife
Measuring tape
Glue and/or hot-glue gun
Painter's tape
Hand saw
Wooden dowel
Construction paper

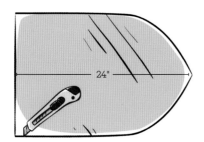

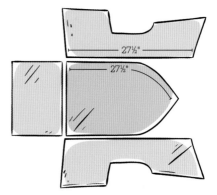

**1** / Draw the base of the ship onto a piece of corrugated cardboard and cut it out. Our example is 24 inches (61 cm) long, but you should make yours a size that will be roomy enough for your cat.

**2** / Measure the outside curve of the base of the ship. The base of your sides will need to be the same length. Our example is 27½ inches (70 cm). The back of the ship should be as long as the base of the bottom and as tall as the sides. Draw the sides and the back of the ship, and cut them out.

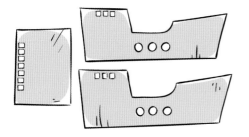

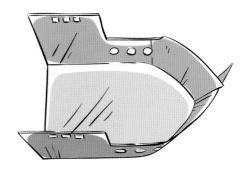

**3** / Cut out portholes and railings, and add any other details you like.

**4** / Glue the sides to the base.

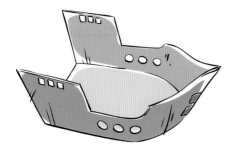

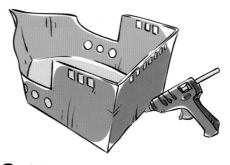

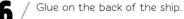

**5** / Glue the front seam closed. You may have to curve or bend the cardboard to get the edges to meet. You can use painter's tape to hold it together while you glue.

**6** / Glue on the back of the ship.

Cardboard and water—not to mention cats and water—don't mix well, so it's probably best to stay on dry land!

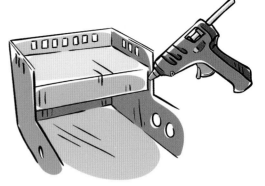

**7** / Measure and cut a piece of cardboard to create the top of the cabin. Glue it in.

**8** / Cut and attach the front edge of the cabin. It should be big enough to support the mast, but leaving an opening at the bottom creates a hangout spot for your cat.

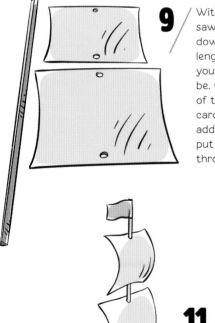

**9** / With the hand saw, trim the dowel to the length you want your mast to be. Cut sails out of the thin cardboard, and add holes to put the dowel through.

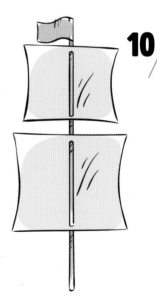

**10** / Thread the sails onto the dowel, and add a colorful flag made of construction paper.

**11** / Glue the mast onto the front of the cabin. Or make a hole in the top of the cabin to poke the mast through. Glue it in place.

Ahoy! Your kitty corsair is ready to set sail!

Here's a **hideout** that is sure to make your cat feel **regal** and **serene,** like the **royal being** she is.

# PYRAMID

## Tools & Materials

Cardboard for template
Corrugated cardboard
Long steel ruler
Pencil
Utility knife
Tape
Glue and/or hot-glue gun
Optional: paintbrush and paint or decorative paper
Small blanket or pillow

Warning! Too small a hole = stuck cat!

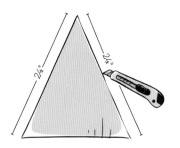

**1** / On a piece of cardboard, draw an isosceles triangle. Roughly 24 inches (61 cm) on each matching side works well, depending on the size of your cat. Cut this out to use as a template.

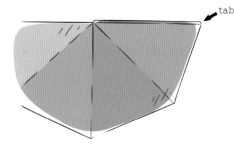

tab

**2** / On a large piece of corrugated cardboard, trace four triangles joined side by side to make the walls of the pyramid. On one of the sides, draw a tab to use for gluing.

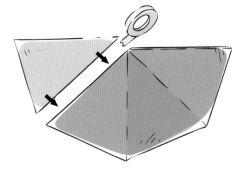

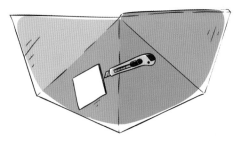

**3** / Cut out the whole shape. If you don't have a piece of cardboard big enough, you can cut separate triangles and tape them together.

**4** / In one of the triangles, cut a door big enough for your cat to fit through.

**5** / Lightly score along the lines using a ruler and utility knife, and fold into a pyramid shape. Add glue to the tab and glue it to the adjoining side.

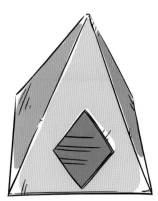

**6** / Decorate the outside if you wish, and add a blanket or pillow worthy of your regal cat's comfort.

When **your kitty** tires of **napping** in a sunbeam, this **clever cover** provides a nice **spot** for a shady **snooze.**

# CAT CANOPY

**Tools & Materials**

Corrugated cardboard
Long steel ruler
Pencil
Utility knife
Measuring tape
Tape
Glue and/or hot-glue gun
Optional: paintbrush and paint or decorative paper
Small blanket or pillow

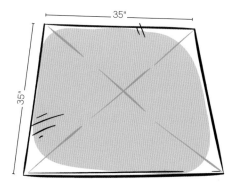

**1** / Cut a 35-inch (89-cm) square of corrugated cardboard. Draw straight lines between diagonally opposite corners, crossing in the center.

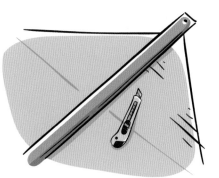

**2** / Using a steel ruler and utility knife, score the lines (but don't cut all the way through).

**3** / Flip the cardboard over. Draw straight lines between diagonally opposite corners, lay the ruler on the lines and fold the edge of the cardboard up, bending along the lines you scored in Step 2.

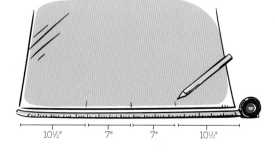

10½"  7"  7"  10½"

**4** / With the folded side up (scored side down), measure and mark the center of each edge. Make a mark 7 inches (18 cm) from the center mark, to both the left and the right. Repeat on all four sides.

**5** / Draw straight lines through the center of the square between marks on opposite sides, as shown. Score the lines with a ruler and utility knife.

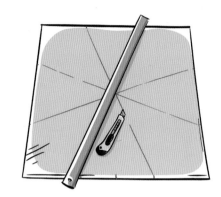

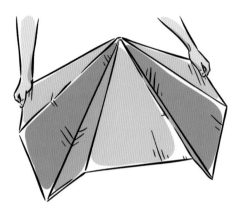

**6** / Flip the cardboard over and repeat Step 4. Draw lines connecting the marks as you did in Step 5. Don't score these lines, though. Instead, lay the ruler on each line and fold the cardboard up.

**7** / Arrange the cardboard in a rotating accordion shape, so that all four corners point down. The lines that run to the corners fold downward and the lines that run to the straight edges fold upward. Set to one side.

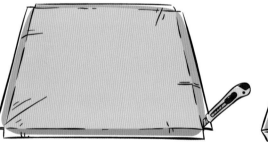

**8** / Cut a 20-inch (51-cm) square of corrugated cardboard. Draw a line 1 inch (2.5 cm) from each edge, parallel to the edge. Score each line and cut out the corners.

**9** / Fold up each edge and tape the corners together to make a shallow box.

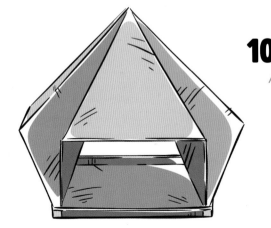

**10** / Slot the bottom corners of the canopy into the corners of the box and glue into place. Now, decorate as you like and add a blanket or pillow inside.

Decorate the canopy so that it makes you as happy as it makes your cat!

It's a **stack** of
**snoozing spots!**
There's **also**
**rope** for **scratching**
and a **toy** for in-between **naps.**

# NAP TUBES

## Tools & Materials

12-inch (30.5-cm) diameter
cardboard tube, 48 inches (122 cm)
long (see page 9)

3 pieces of felt, 18 x 40 inches
(45.5 x 101.5 cm), for outside

3 pieces of felt, 16 x 38 inches
(40.5 x 96.5 cm), for inside

100 feet (30 m) of ¼-inch (6-mm)
sisal rope

Measuring tape

Permanent marker

Painter's tape

Hand saw or utility knife

Glue and/or hot-glue gun

Scissors

Large sewing needle

Short piece of sisal twine

Small blanket or pillow

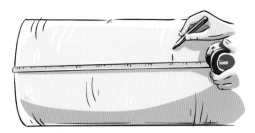
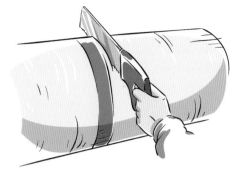

**1** / Cut the tube into thirds: a 48-inch (122-cm) tube will make three 16-inch (40.5-cm) pieces. Make a cutting guide by measuring 16 inches (40.5 cm) from the edge and making a mark. Repeat the process, measuring and marking every couple of inches around the tube.

**2** / Connect the cutting marks with a length of tape to make a straight line around the tube. Cut along this line using a hand saw or utility knife. Measure and cut the remaining piece to make the second and third tubes.

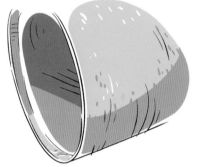

**3** / Glue the 18 x 40-inch (45.5 x 101.5-cm) felt pieces to the outside of each tube. There should be about 1 inch (2.5 cm) of felt overhanging each end of the tube.

**4** / Fold in the felt around the edges of the tubes and glue in place.

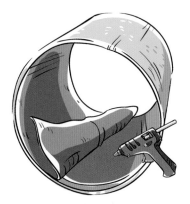

**5** / Glue the 16 x 38-inch (40.5 x 96.5-cm) felt pieces to the inside of each tube. The long sides of the felt should follow the circumference of the tube.

**6** / Stand the three tubes on end and group them together. Wrap the sisal rope around the tubes, pull tightly, and tie a knot to secure them together. Add a drop of glue to the knot to prevent slipping or fraying.

**7** / Wrap the rest of the rope around the tubes tightly. Tie off the end and add a drop of glue to the knot.

**8** / Set the tubes upright and use a large needle to poke a hole in the top of the top tube. Pull a piece of twine through and tie a knot in both ends to make a string toy. Secure it well (you don't want your cat to eat it).

Add pillows or blankets to one or more tubes for different nap options.

# Add a **luxurious** feel to **your cat's** abode with this **Victorian-style sofa.**

# COUCH

## Tools & Materials

Corrugated cardboard
Long steel ruler
Pencil
Utility knife
Glue and/or hot-glue gun
Rolling pin
Painter's tape
Optional: paintbrush and paint or decorative paper

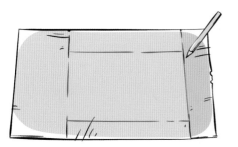

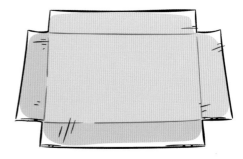

**1** On your corrugated cardboard, draw a rectangle the size you would like the base of your couch to be.

**2** Onto each side of the rectangle, add another rectangle 3 inches (7.5 cm) wide. Cut out this shape.

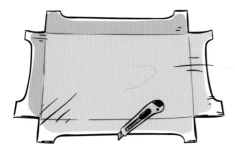

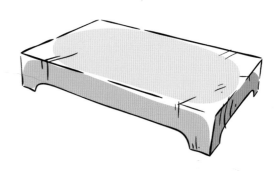

**3** Cut a long, narrow section out of each edge, leaving the corners intact—these will become the legs of the couch.

**4** Fold down the legs. If your cardboard is really thick, you may want to score the lines with a knife and ruler first to make folding easier. Glue the corners together.

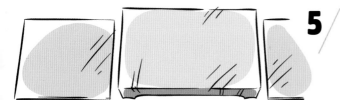

**5** For the arms, cut two cardboard rectangles that are the same width as the base and about 12 inches (30.5 cm) long. The ridges in the cardboard should run parallel to the short sides to make rolling easier.

**6** / Starting at a short side, roll up the cardboard to just past the halfway point. Using a rolling pin can make it easier to get started. Repeat on the other arm.

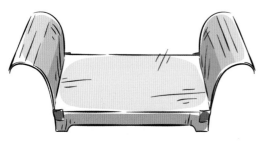

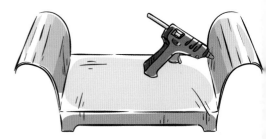

**7** / Tape the arms to the sides of the base to see how they look (make sure you don't cover up the legs). You might want to roll them up tighter, or trim them shorter to get your desired look.

**8** / When you are happy with the way the arms look, glue them onto the sides of the base and remove the tape.

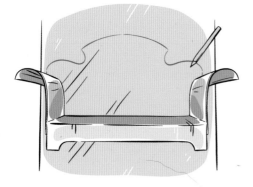

**9** / Lay the arms and base on top of a large piece of corrugated cardboard and draw a shape for the back of the couch.

**10** / Cut out the back shape and glue in place. This is an ideal project for decorating—you could paint it, glue on colored paper, or add a blanket. You can even decorate it to match your own furniture.

Pack a **lot** of **fun** into a **small space** using a **couple** of standard file-storage boxes.

# ENTERTAINMENT CENTER

### Tools & Materials

2 file-storage boxes with lids
Corrugated cardboard for scratching pad and toys
Cardboard toilet-paper tube
Pencil
Utility knife
Glue and/or hot-glue gun
Scissors
Construction paper
Large sewing needle
Sisal twine
Optional: additional cat toys

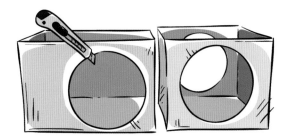

**1** In both boxes, cut holes large enough for your cat to walk through. You can turn one box into a tunnel by cutting doors in both ends.

**2** Cut additional peepholes and windows on the other sides of the boxes.

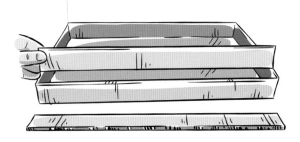

**3** Glue the lid onto the bottom box. Glue the second box on top of the lid.

**4** Take the lid from the top box and turn it upside down. Cut strips of corrugated cardboard that are the same length and height as the lid. You will need to cut enough of these to fill the lid when arranged side by side.

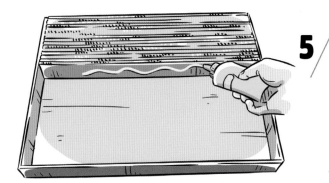

**5** Glue each of the strips to each other and into the lid to make a scratching pad.

 **6** / Glue the scratching pad to the top of the top box.

 **7** / Cut a bunch of small shapes from the corrugated cardboard and construction paper. Here we've cut squares, but use your imagination. Use a needle to poke a hole in each one and thread the shapes onto the sisal twine.

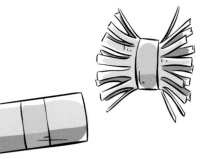

**8** / Glue a strip of construction paper around the middle of the toilet-paper tube. Cut slits into the ends of the tube and bend them outward.

**9** / Attach the toys you made in Steps 7 and 8 to the boxes with sisal twine. Use a needle to poke holes in the box to pull the sisal twine through, or loop string through the windows.

**10** / Add some of your cat's favorite toys and decorate the boxes with construction paper.

Just a few **easy steps** transform a cardboard box into a **cozy abode** for your cat to call his very **own.**

# HOUSE

### Tools & Materials

Large cardboard box, large enough for your cat to fit comfortably inside

Corrugated cardboard for roof

Tape

Pencil

Utility knife

Long steel ruler

Glue and/or hot-glue gun

**1**

Tape the bottom of the box closed, but leave the top open as shown.

**2**

Cut a hole for the door that is big enough for your cat to fit through easily.

**3**

Cut windows in three or four sides of the box.

**4**

Measure the center-top point of the front flap and draw straight lines to the lower outside corners of the flap. Repeat with the back flap. Cut off the two outer triangles on both flaps to form the roofline.

**5**

Fold the side flaps up and in, and then tape them to the roofline.

**6**

Measure the top and one sloping side of the roof. Onto corrugated cardboard, draw a rectangle twice the length of the sloping side and the width of the top. Add 1 inch (2.5 cm) or so on each side for overhang. Cut it out. Use a metal ruler and utility knife to score along the center line to divide into two halves; then fold. Glue on the roof, and welcome your cat into his new home!

**Tools & Materials**

3 cube-shaped cardboard boxes,
all the same size

Corrugated cardboard for details

Tape

Pencil

Long steel ruler

Utility knife

Glue and/or hot-glue gun

Scissors

Optional: paintbrush and paint,
markers, or decorative paper

# Now your space cat can blast off to new heights and leave her paw prints on distant worlds.

# ROCKET

**1** / Tape closed the tops and bottoms of two of the boxes.

**2** / Cut a door in one of these boxes, making sure it is big enough for your cat to fit though easily. This will be the bottom of your rocket.

**3** / Out of corrugated cardboard, cut a right-angled triangle the same height as the bottom box, with a tab on the long side (you will insert this into the box). Trace this shape and cut out 3 more so you have 4 identical fins.

**4** / Cut slots into the four corners of the bottom box at the correct height and long enough to insert the tabs of the fins.

**5** / Insert the tabs of the fins into the corner slots and glue in place.

**6** / On the corrugated cardboard, draw a circle the size you would like the window to be. Draw another circle around it about 1 inch (2.5 cm) larger. Cut out this shape to make the window frame.

**7** / Position the window frame on one side of the second box. Trace inside the frame to create the window shape.

**8** / Cut out the window and glue the frame in place.

**9** / Set the box with the window on top of the box with the door and glue or tape into place.

**10** / Tape closed the bottom of the third box. Cut off the top flaps along the folds.

**11** / On each side, mark the center point of the top edge and draw a straight line from this point to both bottom corners of the box.

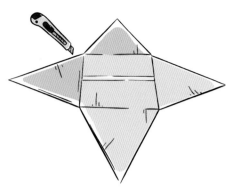

**12** / Cut down along each corner edge of the box so that the 4 sides open out and lie flat. Turn over and, using a steel ruler and utility knife, cut along the lines you drew in Step 11 to create 4 points.

**13** / Turn back over and fold up the points to form a pyramid shape. Tape together along the edges.

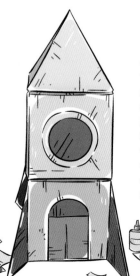

**14** /

Glue or tape the top part of the rocket in place and decorate with paints, paper, or markers if you wish. Now count down to takeoff of your cat's cosmic mission.

This **scratcher** is double-sided, so when kitty wears it out, just **flip it over.**

# HANGING SCRATCHING PAD

**Tools & Materials**

Thick corrugated cardboard
50 feet (15.25 m) of ¼-inch (6-mm) sisal rope
Long steel ruler
Pencil
Utility knife
Hot-glue gun
Wood glue
Scissors

Simply hang your scratching pad on a door handle—unless kitty has other ideas!

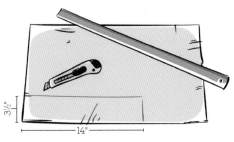

**1** Measure and cut a rectangle of corrugated cardboard that is about 14 x 3½ inches (35.5 x 9 cm).

**2** Glue this rectangle onto another piece of corrugated cardboard and cut around it so you now have a rectangle of double thickness. Keep gluing and cutting until you have a stacked rectangle that is about ¾ inch (2 cm) deep.

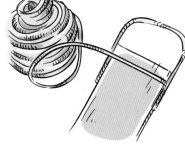
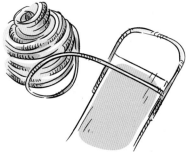

**3** Cut off a piece of rope about 12 inches (30.5 cm) long. Using the hot-glue gun, glue the ends of the rope to the sides of the cardboard rectangle near the top to make the handle.

**4** Using the glue gun, glue the end of the remaining rope to the cardboard near the top. This will hold the end in position while you glue the rest of the rope in place with the wood glue, which will provide a stronger bond between the rope and cardboard but takes a while to dry.

**5** Wrap the rest of the cardboard with the rope, gluing each row with wood glue as you go. Push each row snugly against the previous one to make a solid scratching surface.

**6** When you reach the end of the board, glue the last row using the glue gun and trim the end. Let the wood glue dry for 48 hours, and then it's ready for scratching!

Use **simple techniques** to **create** an amazing-looking structure your cat will **love.**

# PLEATED TUNNEL

**Tools & Materials**

Corrugated cardboard, at least 30 inches (76 cm) square plus additional for the base (optional)

Long steel ruler

Pencil

Utility knife

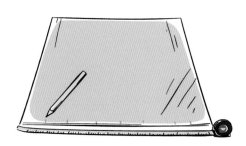

**1** / Cut a 30-inch (76-cm) square of corrugated cardboard. Measure and mark out 8 equal strips. Gently score along these pencil lines using a steel ruler and utility knife, making sure not to cut all the way through.

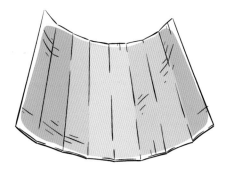

**2** / Flip the cardboard over and fold up along each of the scored lines. You want to crease the cardboard so that you can clearly see your 8 sections.

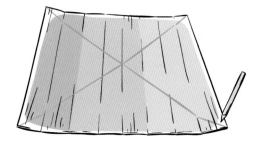

**3** / Draw straight lines between diagonally opposite corners, crossing in the center to form an "X."

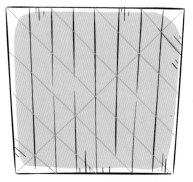

**4** / Where the 2nd, 4th, and 6th pencil lines meet the top and bottom edges, draw lines at a 45-degree angle in one direction. They should run parallel to one side of your "X" as shown.

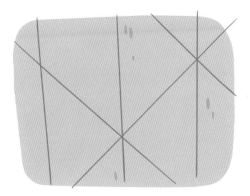

After Step 4, your angled lines should hit the points where the arm of the big "X" crosses the vertical dividing lines, forming more "X"s.

Place the tunnel on a fluffy carpet and you'll have one cozy, happy cat.

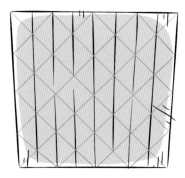

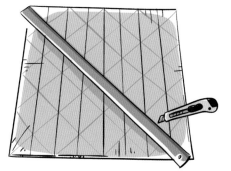

**5** Draw 45-degree-angle lines from the same points, but in the other direction. You should now have a grid of "X"s crossing your vertical dividing lines.

**6** Score along all of the 45-degree-angled lines with a steel ruler and utility knife, but be careful not to cut all the way through.

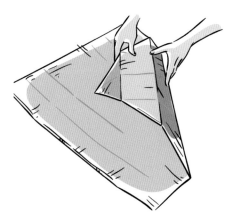

**7** Turn the cardboard over and fold up and crease along each of the angled lines that you scored.

**8** Turn the cardboard over again so that the scored "X"s are facing up. Gently lift the cardboard from the sides that are parallel to the vertical pencil lines. The tunnel should curve, and each cross-point should point outward.

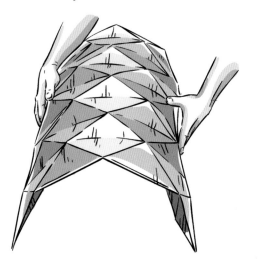

**9** Push the bottom edges of the tunnel together to form a tighter shape. The tunnel should hold its own shape if sitting on carpet and can be folded flat for storage. Alternatively, you can glue it to a cardboard base to make the tunnel hold its shape permanently.

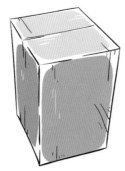

**1** / Choose a box to be the cab of the train and glue closed the top and bottom. Stand it on end so it is taller than it is wide.

**2** / On the other box, which will be the front of the train, glue the bottom closed. At the top of the box, use the utility knife to slice down about 2 inches (5 cm) into each corner.

**Your feline friend can be the engineer of this old-fashioned train, riding the rails near and far.**

# LOCOMOTIVE

**Tools & Materials**

2 rectangular cardboard boxes, the same width and large enough for your cat to hang out in
Corrugated cardboard
Cardboard toilet-paper tube
Glue and/or hot-glue gun
Utility knife
Long steel ruler
Pencil

**3** / Glue closed the flaps of the long sides of the box. Cut the flaps on the short sides into matching arch shapes.

**4** / Cut a piece of corrugated cardboard the same length as the box and about 2 inches (5 cm) wider. The ridges of the cardboard should run parallel to the length of the box (i.e., front to back).

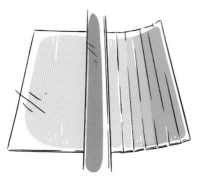

**5** / Using the steel ruler, make creases in the cardboard every inch (2.5 cm) running along its length.

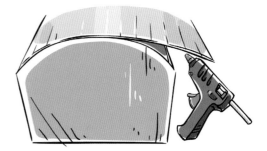

**6** / Starting at one side, carefully glue this piece onto the curved top flaps of the front box using a glue gun.

**7** / Once you have glued the whole thing down, trim the edges if necessary.

**8** / Glue the toilet-paper tube onto the curved top to make a smokestack.

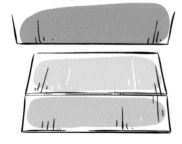

**9 /** For the cow-catcher, cut a piece of corrugated cardboard about 7 inches (18 cm) tall and just slightly narrower than the front of the train. About 3 inches (7.5 cm) up from the bottom, score and fold a line all the way across.

**10 /** Cut out a series of rectangles in the top portion to create a grill.

**11** / Fold the bottom portion under and glue the cow-catcher onto the front of the train.

**12** / Set the cab against the front of the train to judge where you will want the windows. Draw and cut windows in the front and sides of the cab.

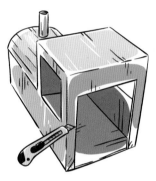

**13** / Cut out a big door in the back of the cab. Make sure it is large enough for your cat to fit through easily.

**14** / On the sides where the front of the train and the cab meet, cut matching doors so your cat can get into the cozy front section.

**15** / Glue the front of the train and the cab together, making sure to align the doors.

**16** / Cut 4 wheels out of corrugated cardboard for the front section, and 2 larger wheels for the cab, and glue in place. Now your cardboard train is ready for a furry engineer to climb aboard.

This **geometric** dome captures **your cat's** multifaceted personality. (Get it?)

# GEO POD

**Tools & Materials**

Cube-shaped cardboard box large enough for your cat to hang out in—about 16 inches (40.5 cm) tall

Corrugated cardboard

Glue

Long steel ruler

Pencil

Utility knife

Optional: paintbrush and paint or decorative paper

Small blanket or pillow

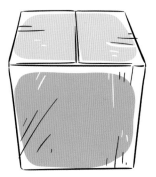

**1** / Glue the flaps of your box closed.

**2** / On all 12 edges of the box, find the center point and make a mark 1 inch (2.5 cm) on either side of this point so that you have a 2-inch (5-cm) space in the middle of each edge.

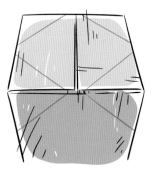

**3** / Connect the marks so that you draw a triangle around each corner, as shown.

**4** / Using a metal ruler and utility knife, cut out the 4 corner triangles on the top half of the box. (If you cut out all 8 corners at the same time your box may be too wobbly to work with.)

**5** / Set each open corner on a piece of corrugated cardboard and trace around.

**6** / Cut out each of the triangles and glue in place to close the open corners.

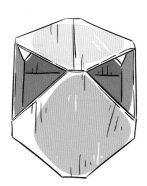

**7** / Flip the box over and cut out the other 4 corners.

**8** / Trace and cut the triangles for these 4 corners and glue in place.

**9** / Cut a nice big hole in the front of the geo pod for a door, making sure your cat can easily fit through. Now your dome is ready to customize—decorate it, add a pillow or blanket inside, or maybe cut out some windows.

This **luxury** condo includes **three different** compartments for your cat to **hang out in,** plus a **scratching post** underneath.

# STEPPED CONDO

**Tools & Materials**

3 cardboard boxes, each large enough for your cat to hang out in

1 cardboard shipping tube, at least as tall as the 3 boxes when stacked

100 feet (30 m) of ¼-inch (6-mm) sisal rope

Hot-glue gun

Tape

Measuring tape

Painter's tape

Pencil

Hand saw or utility knife

Wood glue

Optional: paintbrush and paint, markers, or construction paper

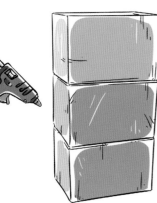

**1** / Hot glue or tape the tops and bottoms of the boxes closed. Stack the 3 boxes.

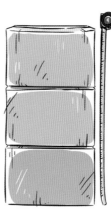

**2** / To find the right length for your tube, measure the height of the stack of boxes and subtract about ¼ inch (6 mm) to allow for the thickness of the top of the top box.

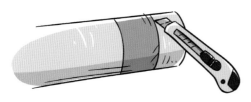

**3** / Measure and mark the correct length on your cardboard tube at several points around the circumference, then connect the marks with painter's tape to make a cutting line. Using a small hand saw or utility knife, cut along this line to trim the tube to the correct length.

**4** / Take the top box and turn it upside down. Trace around the circumference of the tube onto the bottom of the box at the center of one short edge. Cut out this circle.

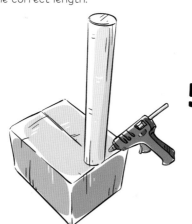

**5** / Apply glue around the trimmed end of the tube and insert it into the hole. Push in the tube as far as it will go—until the end is pressed against the lid of the box. Apply glue around the seam between the tube and the bottom of the box.

This multi-compartment hangout is fantastic if you've got more than one furry friend.

**6** / Using the hot-glue gun, glue one end of the sisal rope to the tube where it meets the box. This will hold the end in place while you apply the wood glue.

**7** / Apply wood glue to the first few inches of the tube. Wood glue forms a better bond between the rope and cardboard than hot glue but takes a while to dry. Wind the rope around the tube, pulling it tight and making sure that each row is pressed close to the last one.

**8** / Continue applying wood glue and winding the rope until you reach the end of the tube. Trim the rope to the right length and glue down the end with the hot-glue gun.

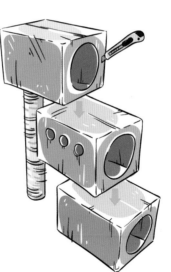

**9** / Cut doors in the front of each box, making sure the openings are large enough for your cat to fit through easily. Add some windows on the sides of one or more of the boxes.

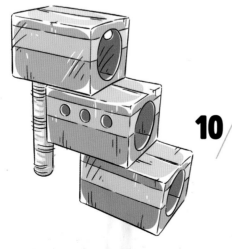

**10** / Stack the boxes in a stepped pattern, with the scratching post at the back, and glue together. Decorate the condo any way you like, using paint, markers, or colorful construction paper.

Turn **cardboard** scraps into something your **cat** **will enjoy** and keep his **claws** in shape.

# SCRAP SCRATCHING POST

## Tools & Materials

12-inch (30.5-cm) square piece of plywood

½-inch (1.3-cm) diameter (minimum) wooden dowel, 30-32 inches (76-81.5 cm) long

Lots of scrap corrugated cardboard

Drill with drill bit the same diameter as wooden dowel

Wood glue

Long steel ruler

Pencil

Utility knife

**1** Drill a hole for the dowel in the center of the plywood.

**2** Glue the dowel into the hole and allow to dry completely.

**3** Measure out grids of 4-inch (10-cm) squares on the corrugated cardboard. In the center of each square, cut a hole the size of the dowel. You can make square holes with a utility knife or use the drill to make round holes. Cut out the squares.

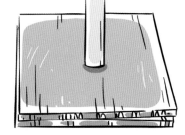

**4** Slide the squares onto the dowel, gluing between each one. You can glue them in a straight stack or slightly offset each square to build a spiral.

**5** Continue stacking and gluing until you reach the top of the dowel. Let the glue dry completely, and then let your cat enjoy scratching!

This **sub** is the **perfect** vehicle for an **undersea expedition**— or just a **nap**.

# SUBMARINE

## Tools & Materials

Cube-shaped corrugated cardboard box large enough for your cat to fit comfortably inside
Small cardboard box, such as a tissue box
2 cardboard toilet-paper tubes
Corrugated cardboard for fins
Thin cardboard for propeller
Long steel ruler
Pencil
Utility knife
Glue and/or hot-glue gun

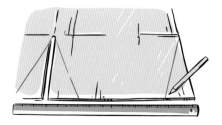

**1** Open the box flaps and flatten the box. On the outer edge of each flap, make a mark about 3 inches (7.5 cm) in from each edge. Draw a line from each of these marks to the nearest inside corner of the flap.

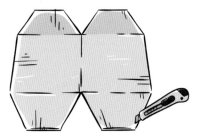

**2** Cut out these triangles using a utility knife and steel ruler. Repeat for all 8 flaps.

**3** Open the box and fold in the flaps on one end until they touch each other. Glue the seams together. Repeat at the other end.

**4** Cut out a circular door in the side. On your corrugated cardboard, draw another circle the same size, then a larger circle around it. Cut out this shape and glue it around the door to make a window frame.

**5** / Measure and draw or trace each end of the submarine onto the corrugated cardboard. Cut out these rectangles and glue them in place to close the ends.

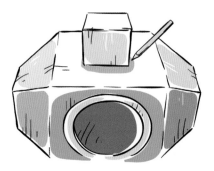

**6** / Set your small box on top of the submarine, right in the center. Trace the shape of the box onto the top of the sub.

**7** / Cut a hole in the top of the sub that is slightly smaller than the guidelines for the small box.

**8** / On the bottom of the small box, cut out a hole that is slightly smaller than the bottom of the box.

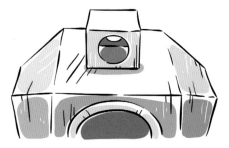

**9** / Cut out circular windows in the front and sides of the small box. Glue it onto the top of the sub, making sure to line up the rectangular holes.

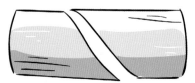

**10** / Cut one of the toilet-paper tubes through the middle at a 45-degree angle.

**11** / Glue the two halves of the tube back together, point to point, to form an "L" shape. Glue this on top of the small box, pointing forward to make a periscope.

**12** / For extra detail, cut out 3 fin shapes from the corrugated cardboard. Glue one of these on each side of the sub at the back, and one on the underside.

**13** / To make a propeller, trace the end of the other toilet-paper tube onto the thin cardboard. Draw 4 fan blades around this circle and cut out.

**14** / Curl up the left side of each blade to give the propeller a fan shape.

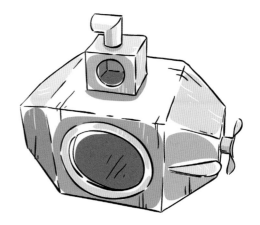

**15** / Cut a slice off the end of the toilet-paper tube and glue it to the center of the propeller. Glue this to the center back of the sub.

**16** / Your submarine is finished and ready to decorate any way you like. Or just hand it over to your kitty and let the deep-sea adventure begin!

# Meet the Models

We would like to say a huge thank-you to our feline friends and their human families for helping with this book. And many thanks to the photographers, Liz Coleman and Phil Wilkins, for their ingenuity, creativity, and patience.

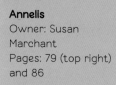

**Apu**
Owner: Clara and Steven
Pages: 29 and 42

**Holly**
Owner: Clare Earthey
Pages: 34 and 95

**Annelis**
Owner: Susan Marchant
Pages: 79 (top right) and 86

**Huckleberry**
Owner: Clare Earthey
Pages 4 (top), 11, 49, 50 (top), and 63

**Belle**
Owner: Susan Marchant
Pages: 4 (bottom), 19, 79 (top left), 87 (center), and 90

**Jasper**
Owner: Clare Abrahams
Pages: 72, 74, and 84

**Gracie**
Owner: Clare Earthey
Pages: 48 and 65 (bottom)

**Jasper**
Owner: Katherine Shone
Pages 23, 44, and 68

**Hattie**
Owner: Tracy Cobbold
Pages: 5, 6, 30, 33, 52, and 55

**Kenzo**
Owner: Carla MacFarlane
Pages: 2, 15, 58 and 60

**Link & Lyric**
Owner: Rozi Blair
Pages: 66, 80, and 82

**Percy**
Owner: Katherine Shone
Pages: 20, 23, and 47

**Salazar**
Owner: Alice Parkinson
Pages: 6 (top), 70, 76, and 78

**Remy**
Owner: Michelle Marchant
Page: 37

**Luna**
Owner: Alix Taylor
Page: 24

**Sokkie**
Owner: Ronel Oberhoizer-Rein
Pages: 10, 38, 40, and 56

**Little H**
Owner: Clare Earthey
Pages 36, 50 (bottom), 62, 65 (top), and 96

**Romana**
Owner: Scarlett Ward
Pages: 3, 4 (center), 18, 27 (top), and 28

**Orphelia**
Owner: Susan Marchant
Pages: 12, 79 (bottom and top center), and 87 (left and right)

**Vivi**
Owner: Alix Taylor
Pages: 17 and 27 (bottom)

# Index

# Credits

Quarto would like to thank the following for kindly supplying images for inclusion in this book:

Lubava, Shutterstock.com, p.1, p. 17 (bottom)
Ermolaev Alexander, Shutterstock.com, p. 8

All other images are the copyright of Quarto Publishing plc. While every effort has been made to credit contributors, Quarto would like to apologize should there have been any omissions or errors— and would be pleased to make the appropriate correction for future editions of the book.